21st CENTURY CITIZEN

World Hunger

Steven Maddocks

FRANKLIN
WATTS

Titles in this series:
AIDS
Animal Rights
Genetic Engineering
Immigrants and Refugees
Terrorism
World Hunger

© 2004 Arcturus Publishing Ltd

Produced for Franklin Watts by
Arcturus Publishing Ltd, 26/27 Bickels Yard,
151-153 Bermondsey Street, London SE1 3HA.

Series concept: Alex Woolf
Editor: Kelly Davis
Designer: Stonecastle Graphics/Kudos Design
Graphs: William Donohoe
Consultant: Kaye Stearman
Picture researcher: Shelley Noronha,
    Glass Onion Pictures

Published in the UK by Franklin Watts.

British Library Cataloguing Publication Data
A CIP catalogue record for this book is
available from the British Library.

ISBN 0 7496 5466 X

Printed and bound in Italy

Franklin Watts – the Watts Publishing Group,
96 Leonard Street, London EC2A 4XD.

Picture acknowledgements
Camera Press (Benoit Gysembergh) 32; Exile
Images 8 and 38 (J. Holmes), 11 (R. Chalasani),
15, 16 and 17 (H. Davies), 18 (A. Ilic);
Popperfoto 23 and cover, above (Danilo
Krstanovic); Still Pictures 12 and title page
(Pieternella Pieterse), 7 (Heine Pedersen), 21, 40
and 45 (Jorgen Schytte), 26 (J. Frebet), 31, 35
(Andrew Davies), 36 (Adrian Arbib), 37 (Penny
Tweedie) 20, 41; Topham 4 and cover, below, 9
(Steve and Mary Skjold/The Image Works), 10,
13, 19, 24 (Kathy McLaughlin/The Image
Works), 25, 27 (Journal-Courier/Steve
Warmowski/The Image Works), 28 (The Image
Works), 29 (Bob Daemmrich/The Image
Works), 39 (Sean Sprague/The Image Works),
43.

Cover pictures
Cover (above) shows a European supermarket;
cover (below) shows a young child suffering
from malnutrition.

Note to parents and teachers
Some recommended websites are listed under
'Useful Addresses' at the back of this book.
Every effort has been made by the Publishers to
ensure that these websites are suitable for
children; that they are of the highest
educational value; and that they contain no
inappropriate or offensive material. However,
because of the nature of the Internet, it is
impossible to guarantee that the contents of
these sites will not be altered. We strongly
advise that Internet access is supervised by a
responsible adult.

Contents

1: Who is Hungry?

Most readers of this book – in common with the writer – will never experience true hunger: a need for food so profound that it destroys mind and body. Yet in 2002 six and a half million babies and young children died from hunger-related causes. Put another way, 18,000 children died every day. Put another way still, five children have died of hunger in the last 30 seconds – probably only a little longer than the time it has taken you to read this paragraph.

Yet world hunger is a problem with a solution. There is more than enough food to feed the world's people and more than enough money to pay for it. Unfortunately, the food and money are not shared out equally. A small proportion of people have far more than they need, and the majority do not have enough.

At the 1996 World Food Summit in Rome, 158 countries signed a pledge (a promise) to halve the number of hungry people in the world by the year 2015. Progress is slow, but thanks to the efforts

This young child's swollen belly is a sign of malnutrition.

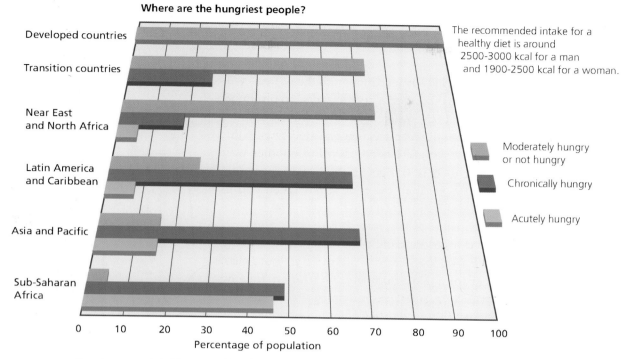

Where are the hungriest people?

Developed countries

Transition countries

Near East
and North Africa

Latin America
and Caribbean

Asia and Pacific

Sub-Saharan
Africa

The recommended intake for a
healthy diet is around
2500-3000 kcal for a man
and 1900-2500 kcal for a woman.

Moderately hungry
or not hungry

Chronically hungry

Acutely hungry

Percentage of population

0 10 20 30 40 50 60 70 80 90 100

Based on a graph in 'The state of food insecurity in the world',
2000, Food and Agriculture Organization website.

of governments, companies, aid organizations and dedicated individuals all over the world, millions of people are saved from hunger every year. With an even greater effort, world hunger could be reduced and even eliminated.

In this chapter, some of the facts and figures relating to world hunger are explained. The causes of world hunger are discussed in Chapter 2, and Chapter 3 analyses the way food is grown and traded around the world. Chapter 4 examines how the world is fighting back against hunger, and the final chapter looks at what the future holds.

What is hunger?

Over the last 20 years, several food emergencies, particularly in African conflict zones, have been recorded by the world's media. Television images showing large numbers of skeletally thin people starving to death have become sadly familiar. This kind of starvation is known as acute hunger. The diet of a person suffering acute hunger is deficient in everything – the body is simply not getting enough food. The daily energy intake of an acutely hungry person is lower than the recommended amount by 400 kcal (kilocalories) or more. Yet acute hunger accounts for

This graph illustrates the severity of hunger in the regions of the world. The mauve bar represents the percentage of the population that is moderately hungry or not hungry, the dark blue bar represents the percentage that is chronically hungry and the light blue bar represents the percentage that is acutely hungry.

only 10 per cent of hunger deaths. The remaining 90 per cent die a much slower death from chronic hunger (or malnutrition), which attracts far fewer headlines.

The diet of a chronically hungry person is 100-400 kcal a day less than the recommended intake. While this deficit is not usually enough to kill a person quickly, the body reacts to this gradual starvation by slowing down physical activity, mental development and growth. The simplest tasks become exhausting. It becomes difficult to concentrate in school or at work. Diseases are impossible to fight off: simple colds may turn into severe pneumonia and a bout of diarrhoea can lead to dangerous dysentery. Those who survive remain damaged for life. If they have children, parenthood is a great struggle, and their children are likely to suffer similar hardships. Many of the world's poor rural communities are trapped in this repeating cycle of hunger.

Three-quarters of those who die of hunger every year are under the age of five. The proportion is so high because children are more dependent than adults on a good diet to remain healthy and to grow properly. Children are also less able to fend for themselves. They rely on others (their parents and their school) to provide their food. If there is any shortage of food, children generally suffer the worst effects.

Where are the hungry people?

In 2002 the Food and Agriculture Organization of the United Nations (FAO) estimated that 840 million people in the world were hungry. About 799 million (95 per cent of the total) were living in developing countries, the poorest group of countries, whose economies are based mainly on agriculture. The developed countries, also known as the industrialized countries because of their industrial economies, accounted for 11 million.

The remaining 30 million lived in countries that were making the transition from the first group to the second. The transition countries consist mainly of Eastern European countries such as Albania and Bulgaria, and former Soviet republics such as Armenia and Kazakhstan.

By numbers, Asia is the worst affected, with 233 million undernourished people in India alone and 119 million in China. However, numbers are falling (particularly in China) and most hungry people in Asia suffer moderate undernourishment (an average daily deficit of around 200 kcal). Judging by the percentage of the population that is hungry, sub-Saharan Africa (the part of Africa south of the Sahara Desert) is by far the worst affected region in the world, with as many as 70 per cent of the people in some countries going hungry. African hunger is more severe, with a much lower average daily intake of calories than in Asia.

Attempts to combat poverty in the developing countries are made more difficult by rising populations in those countries. Since 1960, for example, Asia's population has doubled and Africa's population has trebled. The United Nations estimates that, if the world's population continues to rise as forecast, by the year 2050 nine out of ten of the world's people will live in a developing country.

In the desert of drought-stricken Ethiopia, hundreds of people queue for emergency food aid.

CASE STUDY

Samira Khan lives in an isolated village in the hills of Pakistan. She is 15 and newly married. She lives with her husband's family. The men work all day on a nearby plantation, where sugarcane is grown – to be sold overseas. During the day, Samira looks after the house. She fetches water from a well 3 km away, washes clothes and prepares the meals. Although she looks quite healthy, she is malnourished.

In the morning she drinks tea with milk and sugar and gives the men their breakfast. When they have left, Samira eats her share – one paratha (a type of pancake made of flour and butter). Sometimes she has a fried egg. In the afternoon she eats a chapati (a type of bread) with some vegetables and sometimes beans. In the evening Samira serves the men their meal and then eats hers: another chapati with vegetables.

The village is a long way from any towns, and Samira's husband has very little money. Samira depends on what she can grow for food. Her diet is deficient in fats and carbohydrate, and she should be eating more vitamins, calcium and iron. Samira is still young; if her diet does not improve, her body and mind will not develop healthily. If she becomes pregnant, her health and that of her baby will be at risk.

Young girls in northern Pakistan, 1998.

What is malnutrition?

Malnutrition is ongoing chronic hunger that either gradually kills sufferers or leaves them permanently damaged. As malnourished people are generally not emaciated (very skinny), you cannot tell a malnourished person by looking at him or her. For this reason, malnutrition is sometimes known as 'the hidden hunger'. Malnutrition is also known as the 'silent emergency', because – compared with dramatic stories of unforeseen food emergencies – it attracts few headlines. Three-quarters of malnutrition deaths are mildly to moderately malnourished children, who simply fall ill and never recover.

The most vulnerable groups are children up to three, and pregnant women and their unborn babies. Children who suffer malnutrition remain damaged for life in body and mind. If a pregnant mother is malnourished (or if she experienced malnutrition during her own childhood), her baby is very likely to be underweight and weakened for life.

Malnutrition is not just a problem of the developing world. During the 1990s, a US congressional study found that for at least part of the month (usually in the run-up to payday) one in nine Americans cannot afford to feed themselves adequately. In November 2003, a panel of British nutrition experts found that two million people in the UK, including up to 60 per cent of people arriving for hospital treatment, were undernourished.

Christmas dinner is served at a church soup kitchen in Minneapolis, USA.

How long has this been going on?

In early human history, societies depended on small-scale agriculture, hunting, herding and fishing to supply their food. (While this is no longer the case in industrialized countries, people in many parts of the world still farm or hunt their own food). In agricultural communities, when livestock die or the annual harvest fails, the result is a severe food shortage.

Famine was a frequent occurrence in the ancient world. A *stele* (engraved stone pillar), found in southern Egypt, describes a seven-year famine that occurred around 2760 BC. The famine was caused by a drought that substantially decreased the level of the Nile and left bordering farmlands parched. The inscription recalls that 'children cried … The hearts of the old were needy … Temples were shut, shrines covered with dust, everyone was in distress.'

More recently, a potato famine in Ireland (1845-49), caused by a combination of crop disease and inadequate relief efforts, reduced the population of Ireland by around a quarter. During the First World War (1914-18) entire communities, particularly in Eastern Europe and Russia, were uprooted by the fighting and forced to flee their homes. This internal refugee crisis was made worse by a devastating drought in 1921. The general famine that resulted killed anywhere between two and ten million Russians.

People queue for bread in war-affected St Petersburg, Russia, in 1917.

What is being done about world hunger?
The United Nations (UN) was founded on 24 October 1945, after the Second World War (1939-45) had caused even greater devastation than the First World War. The UN made it a priority to help those people facing starvation as a result of the war and immediately set up the Food and Agriculture Organization (FAO). In 1962, the UN established the World Food Programme (WFP) which distributes food aid. The world's biggest feeding organization, the WFP delivers 6.5 million tonnes of food annually. In 2002, the WFP fed 72 million people in 82 countries.

As the number of hungry people in the world began to escalate rapidly during the 1970s, a great many individuals and organizations joined in the campaign to reduce world hunger. Campaigners included companies and organizations, such as

Oxfam (The Oxford Committee for Famine Relief). In the twenty-first century, individuals and organizations throughout the world continue to undertake a huge range of activities, including emergency famine relief, agricultural research and media campaigning. They attempt not only to feed hungry people but also to identify the causes of world hunger. Some of these causes are discussed in the next chapter.

Ethiopia, 2000: A boy stands near the carcasses of animals during the worst famine and drought in two decades.

2: Why are 800 Million People Hungry?

Three-quarters of the world's 840 million hungry people live in rural areas in developing countries, where most of the food is provided by small-scale local agriculture. Small-scale farmers are at the mercy of nature. If the annual harvest is a good one, there will be food on the family's table and perhaps a small amount left over to take to market and sell. The profit can be used to buy seed or fertilizer for next year's crop.

Yet, in many of the regions where this way of life prevails, the annual harvest is often not a good one. Many of the least developed countries are prone to extreme and very changeable weather conditions, especially drought (an extended period with little or no rain).

Natural causes

Droughts often destroy harvests but floods can be equally catastrophic. In the southern African country of Malawi a bumper harvest in 1999 was followed by terrible floods in 2000, drowning animals and washing away fields of maize. Further heavy rains delayed planting of maize in 2001, and severe frosts in March damaged maize that was about to be picked. In 2002 the country suffered a harsh drought. As the April harvest approached again, the scorched terrain and the empty grain stores told their own story.

A period of heavy rain can be as devastating to crops as a drought. Maize rotted in the fields in Mozambique, southern Africa, after severe floods in February and March 2000.

Some experts believe that, in addition to extreme weather conditions, dependence on a single crop is also a significant factor in Malawi's food insecurity. Maize was almost unknown there at the end of the nineteenth century. But, after several decades of government policies aimed at promoting maize (which is a valuable export crop), it now forms 80 per cent of the average Malawian's diet.

The poor 2001 and 2002 harvests forced Malawians to pick and eat the 2003 crop when it was still green (unripe) and even to eat their precious seeds. Other people scavenged for banana roots and wild vegetables. In desperation, some Malawians resorted to stealing from neighbours and digging up each other's crops.

Half of all Malawian men and three-quarters of all Malawian women work in agriculture – and thus depend entirely on the land for their survival. In March 2003 the United Nations World Food Programme (WFP) estimated that one in three Malawians was malnourished. The WFP pledged to provide food for around 3.3 million Malawians.

Meanwhile, realizing it was facing a humanitarian crisis, the Malawian government, together with the WFP and a number of other non-governmental organizations (NGOs), distributed seed and fertilizer during the 2003 planting and growing seasons. Despite heavy flooding in some areas, this action, combined with good rains, meant the 2003 harvest was a significant improvement on the previous year's. Nevertheless, despite all the resources directed at solving its food emergency, the situation in Malawi remains extremely bleak.

Four women, one of whom is four months pregnant, risk crocodile attacks while searching for water lily bulbs in the Elephant Marshes in southern Malawi. The bulbs are one of the few remaining sources of food.

PERSPECTIVES

'Sometimes my children sit outside and cry from hunger. Sometimes they put a pan on the fire as if expecting me to cook. I tell them there is nothing. After that all I can do is sit there helplessly and watch them cry.'

Madyawako Lepu, a mother living in central Malawi, to WFP Malawi spokesman Richard Lee, July 2002

Malawi's experience is repeated not only across southern Africa but in countries across the world, from Bangladesh to Bolivia, where the combination of changeable weather patterns and fragile ecosystems often leads to devastating food emergencies.

Human causes

In fact bad weather rarely creates famines on its own. Weather conditions can make a bad situation worse, and can tip a country from crisis into emergency. However, in the world's most desperate countries, the underlying causes of world hunger – chiefly war, poverty, AIDS and social inequality – are human in origin.

War and conflict

During the second half of the twentieth century the way in which wars were fought began to change. The new conflicts were fought not on battlefields with heavy artillery, as was the case in the Second World War, but in city streets and village markets with small arms. Soldiers killed not only enemy soldiers but also civilians. During the 1990s, two million children were killed by conflict, six million were seriously injured, and twelve million were made homeless.

In the early 1980s, 31 countries were affected by drought. Only five (Angola, Mozambique, Chad, Sudan and Ethiopia) suffered famines. Those five were all in the midst of war. Indeed, six of the seven major famines recorded between 1980 and 2000 were triggered by conflict. In 15 of the 44 countries that experienced a food emergency in 2001, conflict was a major cause. War and hunger clearly go hand in hand.

War leads to a general breakdown in law and order. Soldiers may steal food to feed themselves, or use so-called 'scorched earth' tactics (destroying crops with the aim of starving their enemies

into submission). They may deliberately target food production by bombing farmland, food stores and irrigation systems, and by slaughtering animals and poisoning wells. Alternatively, they may attack agricultural infrastructure by destroying roads and preventing the distribution of fuel, fertilizer and seed. Cities, ports and airports may be shut down. A food emergency is often the tragic result.

As a result of the new conflicts, about 15 million people worldwide are refugees, and around 22 million others are internally displaced – forced to move within their own countries. At one point during the 1994 war in Rwanda, fought between the Tutsis and the Hutus, a million Hutus crossed into neighbouring Zaire (now the Democratic Republic of the Congo) in five days – at a rate of 10,000 per hour.

Young militia gunmen in southern Somalia, 1993.

 PERSPECTIVES

'Famines are, in fact, so easy to prevent that it is amazing that they are allowed to occur at all.'

Amartya Sen, Development as Freedom, *1999*

Refugees have little more than what they can carry – no home, no land, no rights, and no access to water and food other than what they can beg, borrow or steal. A number of international organizations, led by the Office of the United Nations High Commissioner for Refugees (UNHCR) provide refugees with emergency aid, especially food, often through refugee camps. (In 2000, one in three of those receiving WFP emergency food aid was a refugee or displaced person.)

Refugees from civil war in Rwanda cross the Rusumo River by boat to Tanzania.

Income poverty

Wherever you are in the world, food costs money. Even a farmer who eats only what he grows needs money to buy seeds, fertilizer and pesticide. Money is also needed to buy any food that cannot be grown, or to buy food to eat when the crops fail.

PERSPECTIVES

'Four out of five casualties of the new conflicts are civilians, most of them women and children.'

Oxfam Poverty Report, 1995

In the towns and cities of both the developed and the developing world, people grow little or none of their own food, and they must pay for everything they eat.

At the beginning of the twenty-first century, the World Bank ruled that anyone struggling to survive on less than 1 US dollar a day was officially in the grip of extreme poverty. There are currently 1.3 billion such people in the world. Around 40 per cent of all children in developing countries – half a billion in total – live in extreme poverty.

A typical poor family in the developing world endures a life of hunger and illness and is unable to afford education, healthcare, clean water or sewage facilities (to get rid of waste). Many of the children who grow up without life's essentials remain poor for the rest of their lives and they, in turn, bring their own children up in poverty.

Severe poverty in rural areas in the developing world is driving increasing numbers of people into cities in search of menial work in sweat shops or as domestic servants, or even just to scavenge among the waste of richer urban households. A whole new class of urban poor is being created: families with no farmland on which to grow food and no money with which to buy food. As many as 200 million people suffer from hunger in the world's towns and cities.

A quarter of the world's hungry people are the urban poor. In the poor suburbs of overcrowded cities, poor sanitation is a major cause of disease. This girl from the Indian city of Lucknow stands by an open sewer.

However, it would be wrong to assume that hunger and poverty are restricted to the poorer countries of the world. Many of the world's richest cities, such as London and Washington, DC, are also home to large numbers of poor people who cannot afford to pay for a healthy diet. In such cities, the problem is not (as it is in Malawi) the availability of food. The problem is that not everyone has access to it. The shelves of a supermarket may be stacked high with food, but what use is that to those who cannot afford to buy it?

It may be argued that the causes of hunger and the causes of poverty are one and the same. Two principal causes of modern hunger and poverty, examined in the following pages, are the global AIDS epidemic and social inequality.

HIV and AIDS

AIDS is a fatal disease that attacks the immune system, and HIV is the virus that develops into AIDS. In 2003, over 95 per cent of the world's estimated 40 million AIDS and HIV infected people lived in developing countries.

AIDS is one of the worst humanitarian catastrophes the world has ever faced and is a significant cause of world hunger. Half of all the world's AIDS infections occur in people under the age of 25 – most of them young parents who leave behind orphaned children. Worldwide, 14 million children had lost their parents to AIDS by 2003. In some areas an entire generation of young men and women has been severely weakened, leaving the very young and the very old to fend for themselves, without anyone of working age to bring in money and food.

A family affected by AIDS is forced to sell whatever it can to buy medicine or food. Agricultural production is reduced because those who would be working in the fields are too sick to do so. Children are withdrawn from school so that they can be put to work or care for the sick.

Whereas many of the causes of global poverty and hunger are linked to government corruption, greed and cruelty, the same

These homeless people live on the streets of Los Angeles, one of the world's wealthiest cities. Although good food is abundantly available in Los Angeles, these two have little access to it.

cannot be said of AIDS. However governments can certainly help fight the disease. If the worst-affected countries commit themselves to educating their people about AIDS and its causes, and if all the world's countries commit themselves to fair and equal distribution of medicines, infection rates could be slowed or even reversed.

CASE STUDY

Chantrea is a 38-year-old woman living in Cambodia, which has the greatest number of hungry people in Southeast Asia. Chantrea's fifth child was ill from birth. He never grew properly and died at the age of two. After her husband fell seriously ill and died, Chantrea found out that he had had AIDS but had been too ashamed to tell her.

Left alone with four children and no money, Chantrea discovered that she, too, was HIV-positive. She moved to the city to try to make some money selling fruit on the streets. Her children scavenged in rubbish bins for anything they could sell. As each day passed, their hunger worsened.

Chantrea and her children were eventually saved by a local charity providing support for people living with HIV/AIDS. They gave her food (donated by the WFP), medicines, basic supplies and shelter. They also encouraged her to meet other people living with HIV/AIDS and to talk openly about her illness.

An AIDS counsellor visits an HIV-positive woman and her children in a slum in Phnom Penh, Cambodia.

PERSPECTIVES

'I was in Malawi and met with a group of women living with HIV. As I always do when I meet with people living with AIDS, I asked them what is their highest priority. Their answer was clear and unanimous: food.'

Peter Piot, Executive Director, the Joint United Nations Programme on HIV/AIDS (UNAIDS), 2003

Social inequality

In the world's poorer countries, not everyone is poor. Many people in developing countries manage to feed and clothe themselves and protect their health. In Mexico and Brazil, for example, food availability per person is almost the same as that in Europe. Yet 23 per cent of Mexico's people, and 30 per cent of Brazil's, live below the poverty line.

In agricultural communities, there is a direct link between the amount of land owned and the risk of poverty and hunger. In Bangladesh more than half of landless rural households live in extreme poverty, whereas only 10 per cent of families owning more than 3 hectares of land live below the poverty line.

A subsistence farmer in the Sahel, an arid region of western and north-central Africa, struggles to grow his crops on poor, rocky land.

Generally, landowners let out plots of land to tenant farmers, who pay rent or give part of their crop in exchange for the right to live on the land. The peasant farmers farm the land but do not own it. Their lives are entirely in the hands of the landowners, who may raise rents, demand a greater share of the produce, or force them to move.

In the mid-1970s the Sahel, an area of northwestern Africa, suffered a terrible famine when harvests throughout the region failed after a long drought. Yet many experts point out that drought was not the sole cause; human actions were also to blame. Sahelian landowners, realizing that hard times lay ahead, had sold off much of the good land to large-scale agricultural producers who grew cash crops (crops that are sold for cash, usually overseas). Small-scale farmers growing food for home consumption were therefore forced onto unproductive land. (For more on cash crops, see pages 26-27.)

In many developing countries there is inequality on a smaller scale – within communities and families. When food is short, not everyone gets a fair share. In some traditional cultures, young girls tend to find themselves passed over in favour of their brothers for food, medical attention and schooling. Mothers and daughters fill their plates only when father and sons have taken what they want (see Samira's diet, page 8).

Yet in rural communities in many developing countries, women are the chief family food providers. In Africa, eight out of ten working farmers are women. It is women who spend hours in the fields growing fruit and vegetables, tending chickens, gathering eggs and feeding

Members of a women's co-operative cultivate their fields of tomato plants in Masaku, in central Kenya.

pigs. In the developing world as a whole, 90 per cent of all food consumed in the home is produced by women – yet women own only 1 per cent of the farmland. UNICEF is particularly concerned about oppressed women, for when mothers suffer, their children usually suffer too. Giving women more power to feed themselves, and protect the health of their children, may

PERSPECTIVES

'Wherever women are in control of resources at family level, in general there is far less malnutrition. Wherever women are oppressed, wherever women are not treated as equals, then you tend to get more malnutrition.'

Roger Shrimpton, Senior Nutritionist with UNICEF partner Helen Keller International

help to break the cycle of hunger. According to the WFP, seven out of ten of the world's hungry are women and girls.

Global inequality

Finally there is the inequality that exists between the countries of the world. At the global dinner table, some countries heap their plates high, while others are left to scavenge around on the floor for crumbs.

It has become customary to think of the world as a single community, brought closer together than ever before by the technological advances of the last century. A person can now travel across the world in a day, while at the beginning of the twentieth century it would have taken months. And, thanks to the Internet, information can cross the world in an instant.

Yet the 'global village' is characterized by gross inequality. The poorest 57 per cent of the world's population (around 3.4 billion people) have the same amount of money as the richest 1 per cent. The UN ranks the wealth of nations according to a human development index, which takes into account a range of factors, including poverty, education and life expectancy. In Norway, at

PERSPECTIVES

'Some 54 countries are poorer now than in 1990. In 21 [countries], a larger proportion of people is going hungry. In 14, more children are dying before age five. In 12, primary school enrolments are shrinking. In 34, life expectancy has fallen.'

United Nations Human Development Report, 2003

Shoppers in Europe, the USA and other developed countries are used to having a wide choice of food.

the top of the list, life expectancy at birth is 78.7 years, there is 100 per cent literacy, and annual income per head is just under $30,000 (about £18,200). At the other end of the scale, a newborn child in Sierra Leone will be lucky to reach his or her thirty-fifth birthday, has a one in three chance of learning to read and write, and is likely to have an income of $470 a year.

Ensuring a regular supply of good food, whether in an emergency or not, requires money. In the short term, good roads, refrigerated transport and storage facilities and a sufficient flow of cash are needed. In the long term, generations of farmers must be educated, supported and equipped and the country's economy must be strong and healthy enough to endure depressions without large numbers of people being plunged into poverty – and hunger.

DEBATE

What are the major causes of world hunger? If you were the head of the United Nations, which one would you tackle first?

3: World Food Supply

As we have seen, hunger is not so much caused by food being unavailable as by people lacking access to it. Because of the way food is traded around the world, some people do not even have access to the food they grow themselves. For example, in the early 1990s around 80 per cent of malnourished children in the developing world lived in countries that produced a surplus of food. However, too much of it was exported overseas and not enough of it kept for home consumption.

World supermarket

Free trade is trade in which market forces alone govern what is bought and sold and at what price. Without government interference, producers sell their goods at the best price they can get and purchasers buy goods at the lowest price they can find.

Free trade has helped to create the 'global village', in which goods can supposedly be traded easily between different countries as equal partners. However in practice the global market is neither free nor fair because the buying power of the rich nations vastly outstrips that of the poorest. This is why large quantities of food flow out of the developing world and into the developed world, while comparatively little flows in the opposite direction.

The shelves of this New York supermarket are stacked high with food from all over the world.

PERSPECTIVES

'If the EU is serious about development and less driven by short-term commercial interests, its trade policy should be the exact opposite of what it is at present: it would allow developing-country products into its markets, and it would allow developing-country governments to help their national industries and farmers by offering some protection against competition from the advanced economies.'

Oxfam (The Oxford Committee for Famine Relief)

For instance, even though many Peruvians suffer health problems caused by eating too little protein, much of the protein-rich fish caught in Peru's Pacific waters is sold to North American pet food manufacturers. According to the rules of the free market, Peruvian producers must find the most profitable outlet for their fish. So if an American pet owner can pay more to feed his cat than a Peruvian mother can pay to feed her baby, the cat will get fed and the baby will go hungry.

Fishermen on Lake Titicaca in Peru. A quarter of Peru's population is classified as extremely poor, living on less than 1 US dollar a day.

A free market should allow the Peruvian fishermen themselves to earn enough money from the sale of their fish to pay for other protein-rich foods. However, in Peru excessive state control means that much of the income they earn goes to the government instead. This means that the hoped-for 'trickle-down' effect – whereby the money earned from sales would find its way back to the fishermen – has not happened. The American pet food companies spend a lot of money storing, transporting, processing and distributing the fish and pay only a low price for the raw material.

The experience of the Peruvian fishermen is very similar to that of farmers across the world. For example, the average banana farmer in Honduras receives only 5 per cent of what a shopper in a European or American supermarket pays for a banana. In this way, the poorest people stay poor. And, having been encouraged to farm for profit rather than consumption, they are left with too little food to eat.

Cash cropping

Poorer countries need to compete with each other, producing food as cheaply as possible in order to keep costs low and attract purchasers. They often do this by specializing in producing food to be exported. Food that is grown to be sold abroad, rather than to be eaten at home, is known as a cash crop.

A coffee plantation in Brazil.

Cash crops tend to be mono crops (that is, they are grown on their own). In Honduras, for example, vast areas of land are given over to bananas. Cash-cropping can be extremely profitable – 70 per cent of Honduran export earnings come from bananas. Even if enough of the money does trickle down to the farmers, cash-cropping can be financially risky. The high prices may encourage new producers to enter the market. If too much of a certain crop is produced, the market becomes saturated, and prices fall.

Even when cash-cropping does make economic sense, it is not the best way of using land and can leave farmers very vulnerable. Pests and blights tend to attack one specific crop and will quickly infest any single area where that crop is cultivated. Potatoes, grown as a cash crop in many countries, are especially prone to a disease known as late blight. At the end of the 1990s, late blight seriously damaged the potato crop in sub-Saharan Africa and cost the region billions of dollars in export earnings.

Cash crop farmers are taking a great risk by depending so heavily on a single commodity for their survival. In October 1998 Hurricane Mitch swept through Honduras. In three days of floods and mudslides, the banana crop was all but destroyed. Honduras' fragile economic development was set back 20 years, and millions of people were plunged into deep poverty. The WFP estimates that the post-Mitch reconstruction effort will take many years yet.

Intensive farming

There is a growing tendency throughout the world for farmers to adopt intensive farming techniques to boost food production (see pages 35-36). However, although intensive farming offers great financial benefits, it can be environmentally disastrous. Poisonous chemicals, such as pesticides, fertilizers, and petrol to fuel agricultural machinery, are introduced into the environment. Intensive farming also requires a great deal of water. In countries where water is scarce, sources of drinking water may be drained.

If not properly managed, intensive farming techniques – for instance, the chopping down of trees to create crop fields, intense cultivation, heavy grazing by animals – can strip away the top level of soil and turn land into barren, dry desert (a process

Soybean is farmed intensively across the United States. This farm is in Jacksonville, Illinois.

known as desertification). This process is irreversible, and the world's deserts – unable to sustain crops, livestock or human activity – are spreading.

The environmental dangers of intensive farming are demonstrated by the tragic example of the Aral Sea in Central Asia, once the world's fourth largest inland sea. The Aral Sea began to shrink after the two rivers that fed it were diverted to provide water for intensive cotton plantations. The sea is now a fraction of its original size, and once-thriving fishing ports lie miles from the water's edge. Thousands have lost their livelihoods, hunger is widespread and many people in the area are continually dependent on emergency food aid. Drinking water is polluted by the chemicals used to feed the plantation, and diseases (especially tuberculosis and cancer) are common. Although work is underway to slow down the rate of shrinking, it is unlikely that life around the Aral Sea will ever return to the way it used to be.

By switching to intensive farming methods, developing-world farmers tend to become less self-sufficient. To cover the high costs of intensive farming, producers strike lucrative deals with international food companies (and often with well-known supermarket chains). These companies buy in such large quantities that they can dictate what is grown, when, and how much it is sold for. Farmers also depend on the agricultural

A boat lies stranded in Muynak, Russia. Muynak used to be a harbour but the waters of the Aral Sea are now 95 km away.

suppliers who provide better varieties of seed and animal hormones, and the petrochemical companies who sell the fertilizers and fuels without which no intensive farm can be run.

Subsidies and tariffs

While the world's richer countries strongly encourage the poorer countries to free up their agricultural markets, they are reluctant to open up their own markets and subject their own farmers to the same economic forces – and risks.

One reason for this policy is simple: agriculture requires a large workforce, and labour is much cheaper in, say, Africa than it is in Europe. If the market were truly freed up, African countries could produce some crops much more cheaply than in Europe or America. The agriculture sectors of certain developed countries would collapse.

The developed nations, especially the European countries, the United States and Japan, protect their farmers in two ways. They impose tariffs (taxes) on commodities produced by the developing world and they support their own farmers with subsidies (payments).

Cotton being harvested in Texas, USA.

PERSPECTIVES

'Our farmers, who produce ... cotton 50 per cent cheaper than their competitors from developed countries ... suffer the negative impact of cotton subsidies. These subsidies have caused economic and social crises in African cotton-producing countries... More than ten millions of people in West and Central Africa directly depend on cotton production, and several other millions of people are indirectly affected by the distortion of world market prices due to production and export subsidies ... our countries are not asking for charity ... preferential treatment or additional aid ... Our producers are ready to face competition on the world cotton market – under the condition that it is not distorted by subsidies.'
President Blaise Compaore of Burkina Faso, addressing the World Trade Organization, Geneva, Switzerland, 10 June 2003

Several basic commodities, such as coffee, sugar, bananas and cotton, which are farmed in both the developing and the developed world, are protected in this way. Europe maintains a sugar beet industry even though the costs of production are more than double those of, say, Zambia. However, because of the tariffs imposed on Zambian sugar and the $1.6 billion that European sugar farmers receive in subsidies every year, the Europeans can offer their sugar at a lower price than their developing-world competitors.

It may be argued that Britain does not need a sugar industry. The world could buy enough sugar from Africa and benefit African farmers by doing so. But the sugar industry in Britain is extremely powerful, as are food producers throughout Europe and the United States. The governments of developed countries continue to support farmers because voters have a strong political, historical and sentimental attachment to their agriculture.

The subsidies paid by European and American governments to their farmers are so great that many produce huge surpluses that never even sell. European dairy surpluses, for example, have created a 'butter mountain' and a 'milk lake'. The WFP and others do what they can to redistribute surpluses to those most

CASE STUDY

Laurent Dumesnil is the last remaining sheep farmer in the Lubéron Mountains in Provence, southern France. He grazes his flock on 14.5 hectares of pasture and sends them off in the summer to wild meadows. This is an expensive method of farming, and Laurent receives financial support from the French government and the European Union (EU) to help him produce his lamb. Although Laurent is a small-scale farmer whose produce makes little impact on world markets, he is worried that the government will bow to pressure to cut all subsidies to farmers. If they do so, the livelihood that supported his father, his father's father, and countless generations before them, will come to an end. He asks, 'why should world trade rules dictate whether French taxpayers can pay me to preserve our way of life and protect our countryside?'

'We have opened our economy. That's why we are flat on our back.'

Sam Mpasu, Malawi's commerce and industry minister, at the WTO Conference, September 2003

in need, but, as most of the food deteriorates quickly, they face a race against time. Wherever possible, the WFP locates food surpluses in the country or region of the emergency.

The issue of protectionism was debated at the September 2003 summit, held in Cancún, Mexico, of the World Trade Organization (WTO), which is responsible for overseeing international trade. The poorer countries campaigned for a dismantling of trade barriers and cancelling of subsidies. Four West African countries – Burkina Faso, Chad, Mali and Benin – asked the USA to cut the $3 billion it spends each year subsidizing American cotton farmers. This total (more than the value of the four countries' combined harvest) was shared out among just 25,000 farmers.

A bumper wheat harvest, in Kansas, USA. There was so much wheat that it had to be dumped outside the silo.

The world food trade places developing-world farmers and developed-world farmers in direct competition with one another. Some experts, particularly those at the World Bank and the International Monetary Fund (IMF), who are engineering the move towards global free trade, argue that the need to be competitive will push the developing countries forward. Others believe that the competition is one that developing-world farmers have no chance of winning. As one Sri Lankan activist put it, 'free trade is like putting the rabbit and tiger in the same cage'.

DEBATE

Are governments of developed countries, such as those of Europe, the United States and Japan, right to protect their own farmers by giving them subsidies?

4: Fighting Back

The campaign to turn back the tide of world hunger is led by inter-governmental organizations, particularly UN bodies. The Food and Agriculture Organization (FAO), World Food Programme (WFP), the United Nations Children's Fund (UNICEF), the International Fund for Agricultural Development (IFAD), the United Nations Development Programme (UNDP) and the World Health Organization (WHO) undertake a huge range of activities, including raising funds, setting targets and analysing whether they are being met, researching agriculture, health and nutrition, and organizing emergency aid.

They are supported in their work by a large number of non-governmental organizations (NGOs) all over the world, from

Entire neighbourhoods were reduced to rubble when an earthquake ripped through five provinces and devastated more than 20 towns and cities in western Colombia on 25 January 1999.

PERSPECTIVES

'The clean-up of the destroyed towns and communities is under way, but sometimes it seems as though every time the rubble is shifted, a new corpse is discovered underneath ... families are living in tiny huts made from sheets of plastic or cardboard boxes which they have erected at the site of what used to be their home. ... Others are living in tents in parks or open fields.'

Rosa Antolin, WFP Senior Liaison Officer for Latin America, speaking in February 1999, two weeks after a devastating earthquake hit western Colombia

small local specialist organizations to major global campaigners, such as Save the Children and Action Contre la Faim (Action Against Hunger). The cooperation and support of national governments is crucial to the global effort to relieve poverty and feed the hungry.

Emergency relief

A significant portion of the money spent on relieving world hunger goes towards providing emergency supplies for victims of food emergencies. Some of these emergencies are triggered by natural disasters, such as earthquakes.

For instance, on 25 January 1999 an area of western Colombia, in the Andes Mountains, was struck by the most powerful earthquake seen for a century. Within a few minutes, the people of the region were facing chaos, and 158,000 lost their homes. There was no electricity, no running water and no sanitation. The disaster area extended across five provinces in Colombia's coffee-growing heartland. Farmers saw the infrastructure required to farm their precious cash crop – roads, warehouses and processing plants – wiped out in an instant.

The Colombian government drew up a national emergency plan and enlisted the help of several international and local NGOs. Governments around the world, from Mexico to Japan, donated resources, finance and personnel. Tented villages sprang up throughout the region, and – despite a continual background of conflict and unrest – tens of thousands of people were fed and given medical attention. Within a week of the tragedy, the WFP had pledged to feed 115,000 people for six months at a total cost of US $4.5 million.

CASE STUDY

With over 2,000 paid workers and up to 80,000 volunteers, the Colombian Red Cross (CRC) is one of the country's leading NGOs. Immediately after the earthquake, relief workers were sent to the disaster area to set up food distribution centres. The operation in Armenia, one of the worst-affected cities, was overseen by Fernando Betancourt. In continual contact with CRC headquarters by mobile phone, Fernando provided updates on the worsening situation and tried to arrange for food to be brought in as quickly as possible.

Fernando's colleagues in Bogotá were struggling: much of the route to Armenia went through territory held by rebel armies. If food was flown in, the pilots would risk being shot down. Sending supplies in by land would also be difficult and dangerous. The journey was very long and most of the roads were damaged. In addition, the truck drivers would be vulnerable to attack by bandits – who were also keen to get their hands on the food.

On Friday 29 January 1999, the first food trucks finally rolled into Armenia, and Fernando and local Red Cross volunteers unpacked the food and placed it in the Red Cross warehouse. Within a week of the earthquake, over 300 tonnes of rice, beans, lentils, canned tuna, vegetable oil, coffee, sugar, powdered milk, salt and flour had been distributed. For most people in Armenia, life would never be the same, but – thanks to the tireless work of Fernando and his colleagues – tens of thousands could at least attempt to start again.

(Source: Based on documents from the news archives of the International Federation of Red Cross and Red Crescent Societies)

The final death toll of the Colombian earthquake was under 1,200 but it could have been many tens of thousands more. However, although the 1999 earthquake caused particular food supply problems, Colombia has been in social and economic crisis for a long time. Forty years of internal war have forced 1.5 million people to leave their homes, about 57 per cent of Colombians live in poverty, and hunger is a fact of life. Furthermore, food aid is frequently seized by armed groups (a situation common in war-torn countries, such as Sudan, Afghanistan and Sri Lanka). But, unlike major earthquakes, Colombia's ongoing problems do not make for such dramatic headlines, and millions of hungry people suffer in silence.

Improving agriculture

During the 1960s and 1970s, organizations combating world hunger focused mainly on improving agricultural methods in the developing world, and particularly on improving yield (the amount of food that can be grown on the land available).

In the nineteenth and twentieth centuries, industrialized countries experienced something of an agricultural miracle, brought about by the introduction of intensive farming (a method of farming, involving chemicals and machinery, that maximizes the productivity of land).

Because of these high-yield farming methods, industrialized countries experienced food shortages rarely, if ever, despite massive increases in population. Holland, for example, one of the most densely populated countries in the world, produces enough food to feed its own population – with 40 per cent left over for export.

A number of organizations, led by the FAO and IFAD, have campaigned to introduce intensive farming methods to farmers in the developing world. These methods may involve increased use of pesticides and fertilizers, irrigation systems that deliver a constant trickle of water to the soil, and the creation of new

Intensively farmed potatoes growing in Cornwall, in the south of England.

varieties of plant that are bigger, grow faster or resist disease more effectively.

The Green Revolution

During the 1960s, agricultural scientists developed new high yield variety (HYV) seeds. The introduction of HYV wheat, rice and corn to South Asia from 1965 made such a dramatic difference that what started as an agricultural experiment soon became known as 'the Green Revolution'. Pakistan and India, threatened by famine in 1965, were producing enough grain to meet the needs of their population within ten years. In 1979, a grain output of 131 million tonnes established India as one of the world's biggest agricultural producers. Between 1950 and 1992, world grain output increased by 170 per cent – with only a 1 per cent increase in the amount of land used to produce that grain.

However, those who doubt the benefits of the Green Revolution point out that, despite the increase in food availability per person in India, the number of hungry people in India – more than in any other country in the world – has risen and continues to rise. This is partly because the increase in grain stocks has not kept pace with India's rapid population increase. Critics also argue that the higher yields generated by the Green Revolution depend on intensive farming techniques, which come at a high price – especially for the environment (see pages 27-28).

Fighting malnutrition

In most cases of malnutrition, the problem is not the amount of food consumed but the kind of food consumed. A malnourished person may receive enough energy every day (usually from staple carbohydrates, such as cereals and starchy vegetables). However, it is not enough to eat these foods alone. The body also needs regular doses of essential micronutrients (such as vitamins and minerals) to fulfil a whole range of functions.

The planting of genetically modified hybrid maize seed has greatly boosted India's maize production. Hybrid maize has a greater resistance to a variety of diseases, especially downy mildew, that are particularly damaging to maize in southern Asia.

PERSPECTIVES

'While food aid is a tool to support food consumption in vulnerable countries in the short run, in the long run only improved agricultural performance in these countries can increase their food security.'

Shahla Shapouri, United States Department of Agriculture

For instance, a diet deficient in vitamin A can lead to blindness and to serious damage to the immune system – so the body is left unable to fight off diseases such as diarrhoea (which kills 2.2 million children a year in developing countries). Vitamin A is found in meat, dairy products and eggs, fruit, carrots, green leafy vegetables and red palm oil.

In the absence of such foods, just one small capsule – costing a few pence – provides a good dose of vitamin A. At the 1990 World Summit for Children, UNICEF committed itself to the virtual elimination of vitamin A deficiency throughout the world by 2010. It set a short-term target of providing at least one annual supplement for 70 per cent of children in affected countries. In 1998, 27 countries achieved the target. And by 2000, 43 countries were providing at least one dose, and ten of those were providing two annual doses.

Ugandan children wear banners to raise awareness of the need to eat during bouts of diarrhoea. Such education campaigns are an extremely important way of spreading basic medical knowledge in traditional communities.

Food fortification

Another very successful method of delivering micronutrients to those whose diets are deficient is to add them, at the manufacturing stage, to a staple food, such as flour or margarine, that most of the population eats. This process is known as fortification.

Iodine is one vital micronutrient that can be supplied in this way. A diet deficient in iodine (which is absent from food in areas with poor soil) can lead to a range of iodine deficiency disorders (IDD), including slowed physical growth and some forms of brain damage. This problem can be remedied by salt iodization (the fortification of salt with iodine). Salt has been chosen because a person need only consume a single teaspoon of iodine, in tiny but regular doses, in their lifetime.

Salt was first iodized in 1922 in Switzerland. However, in 1990, less than 20 per cent of households in the developing world were eating iodized salt. This meant that each year around 40 million newborn babies were at risk of brain damage because of their mothers' iodine deficiency. However by 2000 about 70 per cent of households in the developing world were using iodized salt. As a result, 91 million children a year were being protected from brain damage caused by iodine deficiency.

Indonesian children add a testing solution to salt to check if it has been fortified with iodine. In 2002, 65 per cent of Indonesian households were consuming iodized salt.

Education

Education is one of the most important weapons in the fight against world hunger. Without education, people lack the power

PERSPECTIVES

'Malnutrition is both a consequence and cause of poverty. Children's nutrition and well-being are the foundation of a healthy, productive society.'

UNICEF web page, 'Nutrition: The Big Picture'

to change their lives. Yet in 2003 around 875 million of the world's adults were illiterate and 125 million children were not attending school.

Education programmes aimed at combating world hunger take a number of different forms. For example, the FAO teaches farmers and fishermen in the developing world techniques that will help them increase their yield. WHO helps fund the education of health professionals, and the World Bank supports schemes to teach local food producers ways of running their businesses that will improve the general food security of their region.

Micronutrient malnutrition often exists in communities where people do not understand the basic relationship between what they eat and their health. By supporting health and nutrition education in primary schools all over the developing world, UNICEF and other aid organizations aim to improve people's knowledge of what is required for a healthy diet.

Children learn about nutrition by playing a game at a clinic in Phnom Penh, Cambodia.

Unfortunately, school attendance is low in many affected communities, particularly among girls. A number of traditional societies believe that girls should remain at home. And most of the 125 million children in the world who are not in school are girls. In Africa, 27 million girls are out of school and in South Asia the number is 28 million. Two-thirds of the world's 875 million illiterate adults are women. Yet, as we have seen, it is more often women than men who provide food and safeguard the health of their families and communities (see pages 21-22).

A mother breastfeeds her child at the Queen Elizabeth Centre, near Harare, Zimbabwe.

Breastfeeding

A number of organizations are involved in campaigns to teach women about the importance of breastfeeding. Many uneducated mothers do not realize that by giving their babies breast milk for the first six months of their lives, they can provide all the micronutrients they need. And in some countries, aggressive marketing of breast milk substitutes has led them to believe that artificial formula milk is better for their babies than breast milk. However, breast milk is not only extremely nutritious but free, and in most cases, it is a far better option for a baby.

Several world organizations are trying to spread this simple message throughout the villages, schools and health systems of the developing world. UNICEF estimates that in Brazil the percentage of young babies fed on breast milk alone soared from 4 per cent in 1989 to 42 per cent in 1996. In Brazil and elsewhere, increases in breastfeeding have reduced infant mortality rates and made countless babies and young children stronger and healthier.

'Triple A'

One key approach to combating malnutrition in the world's poor rural communities is known as 'triple A'. The aim of this approach is to empower people with the knowledge to:
• **assess** their nutritional status
• **analyse** what their diet is missing
• take **action** to solve the problem.

For example, with just a set of scales and a simple chart it is possible to measure the growth of a baby and detect malnutrition before it is too late. After sustained campaigns, especially by UNICEF, local health authorities all over the developing world, from the Philippines to Peru, arrange

monthly weighing days. Families gather to weigh their babies, discuss their diet and receive advice – and, if necessary, dietary supplements. The weighing days are managed not by highly qualified experts who have travelled from miles away, but by the village health workers themselves.

A child is weighed at Rubaga Hospital, Kampala, Uganda.

Breaking the hunger cycle

Ultimately, any sustainable (lasting) solution to the world's hunger problem must involve hungry people themselves. An emergency food package may last a week or even a month, but when the emergency workers move on the risk of hunger may remain as great as ever. Providing new farming machinery for the villagers on a Cambodian hillside may increase production, but what happens when it breaks down, and the only people who know how to fix it are the French engineers who installed it? It is only by planting knowledge in the community that the cycle of hunger and poverty can be permanently broken.

DEBATE

If part of your country was destroyed by an earthquake, how would people cope? Would they be in danger of starvation?

5: What the Future Holds

Between 1990 and 2002, the number of hungry people in the world fell by 2.5 million a year. Some countries, particularly China and Southeast Asian countries, have made rapid progress. Yet the rate of progress is still too slow. If it does not accelerate, the World Food Summit goal (of halving world hunger by 2015) will be reached a hundred years late. What is more, significant gains by a few high-achieving countries mask a worsening situation in many others. If the achievements of the top seven countries are set aside, the number of undernourished people in the developing world has actually increased by 80 million since 1990.

As this graph demonstrates, the number of hungry people in the developing world (shown in red) is falling. However, at the current rate of decline, the World Food Summit Target (shown in brown) will be missed by a long way.

Number of undernourished people in the developing world compared with the World Food Summit target

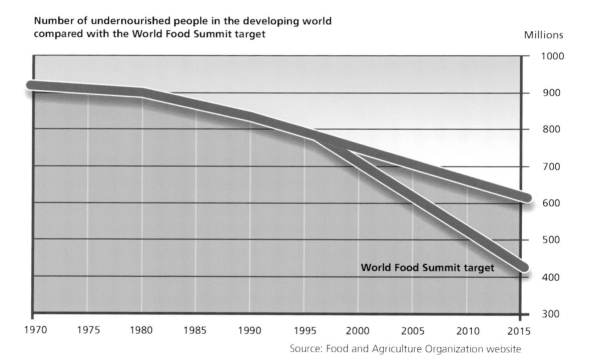

Millions

World Food Summit target

Source: Food and Agriculture Organization website

PERSPECTIVES

'The reasons people go hungry are not mysterious. Mass starvation is not an act of God. Hunger is created and maintained by human decisions... What has been done by some can be undone by others if they use their own strength.'

Susan George and Nigel Paige, Food for Beginners, *1986*

PERSPECTIVES

'The peace we seek, founded upon decent trust and co-operative effort among nations, can be fortified, not by weapons of war, but by wheat and cotton; by milk and wool, by meat and by timber and by rice. These are words that translate into every language on earth.'

Dwight D. Eisenhower, US president, 1953-61

What can governments do?

At the 1992 Earth Summit, in Brazil, it was agreed that industrialized countries should devote 0.7 per cent of their annual income to Overseas Development Aid (ODA). In 2002, only five nations met this target. (The United States gave 0.12 per cent, while the UK gave 0.3 per cent.) Putting a complete end to world hunger could cost US$25 billion a year. This may sound like a lot of money. Yet in 2001 industrialized countries' governments spent $300 billion supporting their own agriculture, while consumers in these countries spent $100 billion on cigarettes.

The impetus for action is there. There is a growing distaste in developed countries for large-scale industrial farming – as shown by increased sales of organic foods. Multinational food producers could respond to this trend by promoting farming in a way that safeguards the environment and protects the interests of developing-world farmers. There is also a growing market for Fair Trade products, whose producers guarantee that the maximum possible profit will find its way back to small-scale farmers. Yet Fair Trade and organic products are generally more expensive than the alternatives, and they still only attract a small proportion of purchasers.

The World Bank headquarters in Washington, DC. The World Bank is the largest source of financial assistance to developing countries.

CASE STUDY

In the 1970s, the German biologist Ingo Potrykus was involved in the development of genetically modified (GM) cereals. Later, in the 1990s, Potrykus led the team that developed 'golden rice', a variety of rice fortified with vitamin A. Half the world's population depend on rice as the mainstay of their diet (many eat little else). Potrykus argued that, if cultivation of rice fortified with vitamin A spread in the developing world, the lives of over a million children could be saved every year.

By 2004, 14 golden rice institutions had been set up across South Asia, but Potrykus and his team were having trouble persuading growers to cultivate the controversial GM rice. A number of international organizations argued that golden rice was not an adequate solution to the problem of vitamin A deficiency (VAD). The reason that VAD was so common, they said, was that poverty had restricted people's diets to rice and little else. They believed that it would be better to solve it by providing sufferers with a more varied diet, which would give them other essential micronutrients at the same time.

Vitamin A is important for sight, immunity to disease, growth and normal development. VAD is a major cause of blindness, especially among children, and it also worsens the effects of measles, diarrhoea and respiratory illnesses. In 2002, the World Health Organization estimated that improved vitamin A nutrition could prevent 1.3-2.5 million deaths each year among children aged under five in the developing world.

Nevertheless, genetic modification remains extremely controversial. Among the chief concerns are that GM crops with built-in pest repellents could escape from farmers' fields and turn into 'superweeds' or could kill other farmyard wildlife. Opponents argue that research into the effect of eating GM crops on human health remains inconclusive. Ingo Potrykus's vision remains unfulfilled.

What can the individual do?

Just by reading this book, you are showing an interest in world hunger – and perhaps even a desire to do something about it. If so, tell other people your opinions. Read stories that relate to world hunger on the Internet or in newspapers, as well as in other books on the subject (see page 47).

Try not to take what you eat for granted. Next time you go to the supermarket, take a look at the label on each item of food. Where has it come from? Who grew it? How did it travel from the farm to the shelf? Pressure the decision-makers around you to change their practices – for example, by buying organic or Fair Trade foods. Write to the press office of your local supermarket chain and ask them how they buy their food. If you think they need to change their practices, tell them so. If you know any local businessmen, try asking them if their companies make charitable donations.

Find out from local politicians how they use their power to benefit the world's hungry people. If you think they could be doing more, why not tell them so? Their job, after all, is to listen to people like you.

Finally, do not underestimate the power of young people to make a difference. By committing yourself now, you may achieve a great deal in your lifetime and help make the world a better place for your generation and for future generations.

A Zimbabwean schoolgirl enjoys her lunch. Will the global community ever find a way of ensuring that all the world's people are well nourished?

DEBATE

Is there anything you can do about world hunger?

Glossary

acute hunger the most severe form of hunger, resulting from a diet that is deficient in protein, energy and micronutrients. If not treated promptly, an acutely hungry person is likely to starve to death.

cash crop a crop grown to be sold (rather than a subsistence crop, which is grown to be eaten). Coffee and cocoa are commonly grown as cash crops, while bananas, maize and potatoes are grown as both cash and subsistence crops.

chronic hunger the most widespread form of hunger, resulting from a diet that is deficient in one or more important nutrients. Chronic hunger leaves a sufferer weakened in mind and body and vulnerable to disease.

desertification the process by which fertile land turns into desert. This begins when the topsoil is left vulnerable to wind erosion by being over-grazed by animals or by the chopping down of trees (deforestation). Deserts spread, and desertification is irreversible.

drought an extended period with little or no rain.

ecosystem a community of organisms (such as plants and animals) that, together with its environment, functions as a balanced and self-sustaining unit. An ecosystem may be as large as a forest or as small as a pond.

fertilizer a substance that provides crops with nutrients that strengthen them and boost their growth. Animal manure was once the most common fertilizer. Modern farmers generally use chemical fertilizers which can have a negative effect on the environment.

food insecurity a condition in which large numbers of people live with hunger, and fear that they will starve.

intensive farming a range of agricultural techniques, often involving the use of complex and expensive chemicals and machinery and requiring a smaller workforce, designed to increase the quantity of produce that can be grown on a given area of land.

malnutrition a general term for the range of conditions that result from a diet deficient in essential components, such as protein, vitamins or minerals.

micronutrient a substance, required regularly but only in tiny quantities, that is an essential component of a healthy diet. Vitamin A, iodine and iron are all micronutrients.

mono crop a single crop planted over a large area in which no other crops are planted.

pesticide a chemical, usually a poison, that controls, repels or kills pests (such as insects, weeds and some birds) that damage plants.

protectionism an economic policy that protects the markets of a given country. A government may protect its own producers (that is, ensure that they sell their produce for a good price) by paying them subsidies that lower their costs, or by placing tariffs on the goods of foreign producers.

subsidy a payment, usually made by a government, that is intended to keep down the price of a particular commodity.

tariff a tax imposed on goods when they enter or leave a country.

transition country a country, such as those in Eastern Europe and the former Soviet Union, that are making the transition from planned to free-market economies like those of the USA and Western Europe.

Useful Addresses

www.wfp.org
The United Nations World Food Programme

www.fao.org
The Food and Agriculture Organization of the United Nations

www.unicef.org
The United Nations Children's Fund

www.oxfam.org
One of the key NGOs working to combat hunger and alleviate poverty worldwide.

www.ifrc.org
The International Federation of Red Cross and Red Crescent Societies
The world's largest humanitarian organization, comprising 181 member societies.

www.thehungersite.com
Award-winning site, a leader in online activism; for every click of the 'give free food' button, the site's sponsors donate a cup of food to hungry people in over 74 countries.

www.reliefweb.int
A project of the United Nations Office for the Coordination of Humanitarian Affairs (OCHA).

www.globalissues.org
A site that discusses the background to some interrelated international issues, including trade, poverty and the environment.

www.thp.org
The Hunger Project
Global movement committed to finding a lasting solution to world hunger.

Further Reading

How the Other Half Dies: Real Reasons for World Hunger
Susan George
(Penguin 1976)

Food for Beginners
Susan George and Nigel Paige
(Writers and Readers, 1982)

Development as Freedom
Amartya Sen
(Oxford University Press, 1999)

The Third Freedom: Ending Hunger in Our Time
George McGovern
(Rowman and Littlefield, 2001)

The following books are all written with teenagers in mind:

Food Supply (21st Century Debates Series)
Rob Bowden
(Hodder Wayland, 2002)

Food Watch
Martyn Bramwell
(Dorling Kindersley, 2001)

UNICEF (World Watch Series)
Steven Maddocks
(Hodder Wayland, 2003)

World Hunger
Liz Young
(Routledge, 1997)

Index

Numbers in **bold** refer to pictures.